MILTON ROW

Robert John Newlands (1922–2003) was a crofter's son from Banffshire who became a teacher in inner-city London, and devoted his career to motivating and empowering pupils from humble backgrounds such as his own. His estate has also overseen the publication of Robert's WWII diary, *Last Letters from Tombreck*.

Note from Valley Press

We acknowledge that some of the language used and views expressed within this book are outdated and occasionally include themes of misogyny and racism. These views do not represent those of the editor, Valley Press or the late author himself. We have elected not to censor those sections as the value of this text may be partly negated by forcing today's principles onto the material. Readers for who such language is triggering or hurtful should be advised.

Milton Row

R.J. Newlands

Valley Press

First published in 2022 by Valley Press
Woodend, The Crescent, Scarborough, YO11 2PW
www.valleypressuk.com

ISBN 978-1-912436-84-2
Cat. no. VP0202

Copyright © Robert John Newlands 2022
Illustrations by Mary Anne Newlands Case.

The right of Robert John Newlands to be identified as the
author of this work has been asserted in accordance with
the Copyright, Designs and Patents Act 1988.

All rights reserved. No part of this publication may be
reproduced, stored in or introduced into a retrieval system,
or transmitted in any form, by any means (electronic,
mechanical, photocopying, recording or otherwise) without
prior written permission from the rights holders.

A CIP record for this book is available from the British Library.

Printed and bound in Great Britain
by Clays Ltd, Elcograf S.p.A.

*For the former pupils
and teachers of
St John's and All Saints School
and John Evelyn School*

Preface

Robert John Newlands was born on 10th June 1922 at a Scottish Croft called Tombreck a few miles south of Keith, close to Auchindachy, on the River Isla in Banffshire. He was the tenth and last child (of those who survived into adulthood) of William Newlands and Jessie Jane Garden. William, as well as tending the six-acre croft, worked for the Great North of Scotland Railway and maintained the track from Keith to Auchindachy for forty years. Tombreck had, as was typical of the time, no running water, gas, electricity or telephone line but the fresh food and companionship more than made up for this relative deprivation. Robert, known as Bobbie to his family, had to clean out the byre once a day and helped carry water from the spring nearby. He attended Keith Grammar School, which was a non-selective school dating back to 1834. Many of Robert's teachers had fought in the First World War, some having been injured in the conflict. They were held in high esteem by all the pupils who came from a variety of backgrounds – from the impoverished crofter's children to the comparatively comfortably-off. William allowed Robert to do his Scottish Higher examinations, much against his mother's wishes, who worried that an education would mean her youngest son would not stay close to his family in North-East Scotland.

After leaving school at sixteen, Robert joined Thurburn and Fleming, a firm of solicitors in Keith, as a legal clerk where he worked for three years. No doubt he would have taken examinations and progressed in this career had World War Two not intervened. On 11th February 1941, aged eighteen, he attended an interview at the RAF recruiting centre in Keith. Though he was initially considered for aircrew, he was offered training as a wireless technician. He undertook a rigorous three-month course in Edinburgh and Bolton, and was posted first to Capel-le-Ferne in Kent and then to Eastbourne in East Sussex. He was in Eastbourne for most of the war at a top-secret listening post intercepting enemy communications, which was sited on the present-day Eastbourne golf course close to Beachy Head. His wartime diary, which is published and titled *Last Letters from Tombreck*, details his life during this period, though because of the Official Secrets Act it doesn't contain any operational details. Whilst in Eastbourne he met Joan Morwenna Johnstone, a WAAF (Women's Auxiliary Air Force) motor transport driver, and they married three years later in 1947. On being demobbed in 1946 Robert took a one-year emergency teacher training course at Trent Park, a grade two listed building near Cockfosters in North London, and qualified as a teacher.

Robert worked at several schools over his career. The one which is most relevant to his poem *Milton Row* was St John's and All Saints Secondary Modern School on Exton Street, near Waterloo Station, London. The illustrations by Mary Anne Newlands Case, an American cousin of Robert's, are based on this school. The building still exists today though it is now an architect's office; it can be visited sometimes during 'open house' week which occurs in London once a year. Of course, the site of the fictional Milton Row was moved a mile and a half southeast of St John's to what was a more deprived area, perhaps also to make the poem seem less autobiographical. Street names like 'Row' were common around the Elephant and Castle district of London before the massive slum clearances replaced terraced housing with high- and low-rise flats which erased a lot of the smaller roads. The 'Milton' of *Milton Row* probably comes from the Milton Tower in Keith. This is the surviving portion of the

Castle of Milton built circa 1480 which Robert would have romanticised about during his school days. Robert subsequently became Head of English at John Evelyn School in Alverton Road, Deptford, although this school has since been demolished.

Milton Row was written in 1963–64 but has never previously been published. Robert's view, because of his humble background, was that poverty was not a factor in the boys' behaviour. This in itself was an unfashionable view at the time. Throughout his teaching career he cared passionately for the underprivileged and felt he could, through discipline and example, help his pupils make up lost ground and make something of their lives.

Robert retired in 1987 and continued with his hobbies of dog walking and collecting Victorian watercolours. He bred from the family labrador, keeping two of the puppies, and used to walk these three dogs twice a day in Lloyd Park, Croydon. That they became part of the family reminded him of life on the croft of his childhood where animals and humans lived interconnected lives. It was often while walking the dogs that he composed his best poems.

He died on 31st August 2003 leaving two sons and four grandchildren, his wife, Joan, having pre-deceased him.

Robert's poem *Milton Row*, published on the centenary of his birth, will resonate with people who lived through the 1960s, but one might reflect that its message is as relevant today as it was sixty years ago.

Biography of Mary Anne Newlands Case

Mary Anne Newlands Case is a Professional Artist Member of The Society of Illustrators and The National Cartoonists Society in the United States. Her past work includes Memory Lane, a daily panel strip, humour cards for American Greetings, and numerous political cartoons. Her writing and sketches have appeared in *The New York Times*. She also illustrated *Rockrose*, a book of poetry, by Menke Katz, which was translated into seventeen languages.

Mary Anne's life has centred on art since the age of six. At The Masters School in New York State she won the Scholastic Magazine Prize for fashion design and a Mademoiselle Magazine fashion internship. Her art teacher steered her to Brown University where she could also study at the nearby Rhode Island School of Design. Over five years she simultaneously took two four-year degrees, a BA in Art and a BFA in Illustration. She studied at The New York School of Interior Design, earned the NCIDQ, and had a thirty-year career in interior design. She later studied Graphic and Web Design at Norwalk Community College for twelve years.

Mary Anne has enjoyed several trips to Italy to paint with friends over her lifetime. She currently chairs a poetry group in New Canaan, Connecticut, USA, where she now lives after many years in adjacent Silvermine, home to artists and writers. She has been told that Robert's great-great-great grandfather and her own great-great-great-grandfather were brothers.

I.

I sing the slums of London and the crime
That's born of cowardice, branding our time
With such a blemish on so fair a face
That beauty's promise and unfolding grace
May fail in flower and fall in barren fruit
Because no courage came at branch or root.

I am of that peculiar wordy breed
Professing knowledge and protesting need
Within the slender artificial state
Called Culture; and twixt warring love and hate
Bled to a shadow, an accepted thing,
A shrine where fear and faith confounded bring
Accustomed praises and accrued neglect.
In short I am a teacher. I correct
Exercises, map out worlds in chalk,
Expound, explain, explode and talk talk talk
From morn to night, from vanished day to day,
From term to term till life is half away
And pimply boys all of a sudden men
And nothing done but must be done again.
I taught a decade in our private schools
Where semi-geniuses and super-fools
Bore one another gladly with a grin
Because their manners served and discipline
Was ever ready to support the weak.
But stucco peels and radiators leak
And rates and taxes soar on kestrel wings
Above a shrinking world of cultured things.

Ministry brick-and-mortar men survey
The narrow window and the worn stairway;
Count up their cubic feet, condole, condemn,
For all that education means to them
Is law and letter: manners, virtue, skill
Were never even mentioned in the Bill.
So my school closed.
                     Thus beggared by the State
It seemed but justice that my future fate
Be in its hands. Was it not vastly proud
To boast of welfare? Had not long and loud
Avowals of the need for education
Been made by every leader of the nation?
Ten years behind me and a fair degree
Would surely guarantee a niche for me.
And so one soft September I was sent
To probe the jungle round the Elephant
Behind the Old Kent Road, where fists are facts
And filthy photos and religious tracts
Fight for the soul; where meths is still a liquor;
Where curses leave the face without a flicker;
Where cups are cracked and foully-smelling fish
With fouler chips conjoin on foulest dish;
Where carpet slippers see you round the town;
Where whores are none too cheap at half-a-crown:
A boozing bingo land of blows and curses
Quite indescribable in decent verses.

As bald and brazen as a conjurer's trick,
Of School Board's warehouse-style in blackened brick
Stood Milton Row, macadamed to the earth;
A seat of learning likely as the birth
Of unicorns and dreary, dish-wash drab.
The doors were peeled and pitted with a scab,
The windows dim and vacant; knots of drains
Twisted and bulged like varicated veins,
And high wire-netting veiled the place about.
A flush of water from a drinking spout
Spread down the yard to seek a sloven drain,
And cluttered dustbins hid themselves in vain
Behind the lavatories which didn't hide
But flaunted basic life with Cockney pride.
A waste of warren entrances and stairs
Confronted me, some single, some in pairs
With 'Boys' and 'Girls' sculpted out above the doors.
I raised my eyes to count the rising floors
And sensed repellent danger and despair
And wondered what strange fate had brought me there.
I took the steps where art's embellishment
Had perched a graven sunflower in cement
Above the door and scribbled under it
Faded, but plainly yet, the motto 'Shit';
And up the stairs, half-tiled in bottle green,
With every window on a London scene
Of mounting drabness, and the sharp excess
Of start-of-term's carbolic cleanliness
Sapping the nerve, and up from floor to floor
Till puffed and humbled by headmaster's door

I knocked and waited as the notice said.
"Come in." I entered. This was my new head.
A little man a little thin on top:
I'd seen him often in a grocer's shop
Buttering the housewives, cutting bacon fine
Or gently pushing sales of some new line.
I was his custom now. "Ah let me see,
You are the man they've sent me for 4B." [1]
And all the housewives voted him so nice;
And I was nothing more than merchandise,
Wholesale delivery, which time would show
To be the stuff that would or wouldn't go.
"I'll take you to your class." He didn't tell
How many more had walked that plank and fell
Amid derisive laughter of the mob:
I had been sent and he would do his job.
But I could tell that there was something up.
I half-suspected I'd been sold a pup [2]
Down at Division, and "You've 'ad it mate,"
The keeper's salutation at the gate,
Was not assuring; but you never know
And I would not condemn this Milton Row
Without a trial. "This will be your class."
The head pulled back the door and let me pass.
A prime selection of low-mouthing louts
And little-witted street-end lay-abouts
Filled up the room and fell upon my view.
They had a seat apiece but sprawled on two
And at my entrance sneered a meaning grin
Articulating, "Now let's settle him."

The head withdrew with greater speed than grace:
I'd seen the smile was hardening on his face
As we advanced along the corridor.
And now alone, a novice toreador,
I faced this surly many-headed bull
And felt in part a martyr, part a fool;
Yet stirring in the embers of my heart
Still glinted something of that dying part
That was my calling and my vision's eyes,
And as a sick man rallies ere he dies
I stood and fought and failed as you shall see.
"Sit up", I snapped, "And kindly look at me."
They half uncurled and clattered desks and chairs:
Admonished, muttering their couldn't cares,
I held at last attention's tenuous thread.
But Bill, in front of me, had lowered his head
Finding a sudden interest in his book.
I paused. "Your book away boy and just look."
"I've 'ad one decko and I've seen enough," [3]
Came the rejoinder, nonchalant and gruff.

[1.] Boys in 4B would be between the ages of 14–15 years old. This would usually have been their last year in a secondary modern school.

[2.] To be "sold a pup" is to be sold something of little worth under the pretence of it being of greater value. The phrase originated from an old swindle where one would be sold a "piglet" in an opaque sack, only to find the animal was actually a puppy.

[3.] A peek or a glance; derived from the Hindi dekhana, passed into common use via the British government's Colonial Service.

And as the forest flame roars up each tree
Each boy became a living flame of glee.
"But felt too little, son," I came back quick;
Lost time was trouble: nip this in the nick
And I might yet save something from the rout.
So ere our Bill knew what it was about
I'd turned the deadly jest and hurled it back
And while he nursed his jaw I joined the pack
And went a-hunting till the play-bell rang.

It takes a day or two to get the hang
Of such a school, find how the system ticks
And whether teachers use their hands or sticks
Or go on nagging till the cows come home.
The textbook tells of royal roads to Rome
Where sympathy makes children grow like flowers
And interest holds their anxious ear for hours,
Psychology elucidates their need
And all the world's a plenitude to feed
Their hungry souls: but when I now look back
To college carriageways, this muddy track
And these endlessly winding rutted lanes
Make me disdain the pundit who remains
In cloistered idealism and fuddled thinking,
And I condone the teacher's trick of winking
When theory's unctuous utterances descend
From prim Ministry mouths, for better bend
Before the wind prevailing at the hour
Than break beneath a temporary power:

When vision abdicates for fashions' sway
Best emulate the reverend man of Bray.[4]
Thus fashions had their vogue at Milton Row.
Gimmicks and gadgets shuttled to and fro
Their home-spun projects of fantastic woof,
With plenteous praise but precious little proof,
Much like the web Penelope contrived,
Forever journeying but ne'er arrived;
And as her trick kept parasites at bay
Do modern methods in our schools today.
The staff was mixed in sex and intellect:
The prime division easier to detect
With women's talk all shop or soiled with self
And men's one long lament on lack of pelf;[5]
And intellect 'twere generous to assess
The most with little and the rest with less.
But courage, patience, willingness to give
Unstintingly, ability to live
The warped frustrations half their pupils felt;
These shone in glory like Orion's belt.

---

[4] A satirical eighteenth-century song, 'The Vicar of Bray', described the titular character repeatedly changing his principles to stay in his post, despite numerous religious upheavals under a succession of English monarchs. The term was further popularized as the title of a comic opera from 1882 and a film released in 1934.

[5] Money or wealth, especially if dishonestly acquired; from the Old French "pelfre" (booty).

Young things with theory dancing in their eyes;
Old maids whose hope of matrimony dies
Only that mothering love shall live unfeigned,
Becoddling Willie when he should be caned;
And then the married train whose worried lives
Of reconciling teachers' tasks with wives'
Lend harassed looks and tangled minds and hair
And that dishevelled haste that apes despair:
Such were the women, and the world should know
The boundless debt of gratitude they owe
To these weird sisters; by the spells they cast
Many a wayward child comes home at last.
The men were something cynical at heart.
They played the role but did not live the part.
The wider venture which the spirit craves
Was somehow lacking, and the faith that saves
Worn thin and shabby: they were like men hired,
Doing what must be done but uninspired
By self-involvement. Most were over-worked
For after every day an evening lurked
In some dim night-school; and a few were bitter
That some advancement for which they were fitter
Had gone to others.
                Presently I learned
The facts and fears by which the school had earned
The designation 'tough', and time again
The story ended with the same refrain
"He didn't stay" or "She was off next day",
Till I grew dizzy with the roundelay.

My predecessors had been far from few:
There had in two short terms been twenty-two
From every corner of the Commonwealth.
"Geezers wot come 'ere for the National 'ealth,"
Was one opinion: "Colleagues helping out,"
The kinder view. The truth was much in doubt,
For any graduate tourist when it's wet
Can always cull a pound or two to set
Against the Spanish trip or Baltic cruise.
One such Australian wench was still the news
When I arrived. She taught arithmetic
The modern way with tape and metre-stick.
But when with floor and table, desk and chair,
All duly measured, one ambitious pair
Observed their mentor and were moved to tape her,
She fled in terror screaming they would rape her;
A booster to prestige among the boys
Whose bragged embellishments brought added joys
To my first days.
                An Indian gent called Din,
And nicknamed Gunga, finished in a bin:
And two consecutive New Zealand wenches
Were tipped unceremoniously on benches
To have their bottoms slapped.
                        A Ceylonese,
Distinguished to the tune of three degrees,
Stayed but an hour, but in so brief a space
The mystery of the vanished leather case
Was stumbled on and solved, or nearly so,
For twenty-five indignant boys said "No:"

The unsuspected swearing "On me life."
The likely culprits swanking, "Find the knife."
And they had something too. No knife was found.
Dismembered strips of leather strewn around,
Some in adjoining classrooms, baulked at proof,
And no-one split but tongue-tied stood aloof
Watching their learned master, grim and glum
And vastly unimpressed with Christendom,
Gesticulate and threaten and depart
With lighter luggage and a heavier heart.
An ex-headmistress from Australia came
For three whole weeks and gained a lasting fame
By knocking cold one boy who'd dared to brag
He wouldn't toe the line for "that ole bag."
A brilliant girl from Ghana, shining black,
Being forewarned was little taken aback
When her appearance raised the nasty titter,
But when a chorus bellowed "Go home sister."
She'd had enough.
                 Thus Education made
A mere by-product of the tourist trade
Floundered amid the rocks of Milton Row.
The calmest deeps have dangers hid below
But these uncertain shores know squalls and tides
With terrors a marine tradition hides
From foreign eyes: and seldom now the strand
That cannot boast a local Goodwin Sand [6]
And scarce the headland free of some sad wreck.
Nor strangers only feared to risk their neck

At Milton Row: the veteran seaman too
Surveyed the flood and tactfully withdrew.
In my short time this human ebb and flow
So blurred reality that there would grow
In me fool notions of superior skill
And scarce concealed expressions of ill-will
Towards colleagues whose sole state-encouraged crime
Was spots of teaching in a sparse spare time.

School is a miniature society
Where all the rich self-willed diversity
Of early life learns tolerance, where grows
Respect within the dance for other toes.
And like a family a class conspires
A single aim for separate desires:
High peaks to challenge, valleys to content,
All in a healthy sane environment.
And should a black sheep haply stain the fold
Fair-play and fellowship securely hold
Back-biting prejudice and pique at bay
And half the battle's won by courtesy.
Only one virtue did my 4B lack:
But for a single sheep the flock was black.

6. Goodwin Sands is a ten-mile-long sandbank at the southern end of the North Sea lying six miles off the Deal coast in Kent, England. Located near one of the world's busiest shipping lanes, it has been the scene of thousands of shipwrecks.

The brightest boy by far was Yiddish Sid.
There was intelligence in all he did
Despite the tiresome burden of his jests.
Quite the most irrepressible of pests,
He'd ruin a lesson with his Cockney quips.
He reckoned Bonaparte had "'ad 'is chips"
The day he crossed the Nieman: "Wot I say
Is ditch ole Liz and lets 'ave Mr K." [7]
He championed Russia in and out of season,
Would darkly hint that some unsavoury reason
Brought "Florrie and 'er birds" to the Crimea,
Opined that generals "ain't got no idea",
And if I dared refute a wild assertion
He'd dig in heels and canvas his own version,
Blighting each flower of fact with withering doubt
And end "'e don't know wot 'e's on about."

Slasher was small and weasel-faced: for him
Knowledge was less a crime than some foul sin
That teachers and such trash might wallow in,
But not our righteous Willie: he preferred
The world of knives in which it was averred
A bigger brother Slasher stood a peer
And kept his local neighbourhood in fear.
My smaller version revelled in his rubs
With coppers, talked with feeling of the Scrubs,[8]
How so and so – the bastard – had been done
And how they nicked the old girl's bag and run.
His eyes were old but they would fairly glow
When he described some underhanded blow

That broke the gang, or how by luck he'd missed
A mighty wallop from a razored fist.
But by that startling paradox of mind
That is the grief and glory of mankind
Our Will displayed a most pedantic sense
Of injury at any violence
A master might be tempted to inflict.
"You take yer 'ands off me. I'll 'ave you nicked"
Came the rejoinder at the slightest tap
That dare disturb his after-breakfast nap.

Dereck had quiet ways and large brown eyes.
He fought the goading world with butterflies
And goldfish, lizards, snakes in grass-filled jars,
Mice and a host of don't-know-what-they-ares
Match-boxed or bottled; and the live-long day
Public and private views of this display
Were sought and settled, and as lessons flowed
Auction and exhibition to-and-fro-ed
In surreptitious swing till someone slipped
And through the floor a precious lizard nipped
Ruining both market and the master's truce.
Who Jesus-like now whipped out bald abuse
And struck for learning, law and purity.
Dereck with all his dumb menagerie

---

7. "Mr K" is Nikita Khrushchev, President of the USSR, 1953–1964.
8. Wormwood Scrubs, a prison in West London.

Departed to the Buildings whence he came
And all would alter and remain the same.
Later I learnt the long arm of the law
Had proved again to Dereck the old saw
That crime won't pay: what crime I cannot tell
But I have hoped there's mice in Dereck's cell.

Sibly was fat and dirty and he stank,
To heaven, a patent fault that lowered his rank
In my fastidious fraternity:
For those who think class is a trinity
Are sadly unobservant: not one street
But twenty fine distinctions shall defeat
Equality, whoever rules the town,
For noses lend themselves to looking down.
But if poor Sibly suffered from his smell
He knew of triumph too for he could spell.
His time would come in composition hour
When gifted knowledge gave him place of power
And troops of ardent pilgrims full of faith
Hung on his every word – with bated breath.

Old Wanker on the clock would come in late,
Set out his books on show and masturbate.
He was a quiet lad, as pale and thin
As any ghost, and always coming in
He'd face each vulgar crack with Stoic calm.
E'er business-like he made his fault his balm.

Fordham was fond of copulative words
And bragged no end of how he'd picked up birds,
Him and his mate, last evening round the cafe [9]
And took 'em down the bomb-site for a laugh.
Fond of immodesty, his special pride
Was how his father spent his days inside
Hobnobbing with the very best in crime.
He reckoned how when he would serve his time
The family name would stand him in good stead.
Of any kind of work he stood in dread.

Jacko was big, and bulk in his world tends
To breed predation and pay dividends.
Soon after I arrived our swords were crossed.
He never handed you a thing but tossed
It with a grunt and studied lack of grace
And at remonstrance pulled a nasty face.
I went for him and told him fair and square
To stop his tricks: defy me if he dare.
"Drop dead," he snarled at me and when I didn't
He raised his fists but quickly wished he hadn't,
For in an instant he was on his back
And didn't quite know how. "That's judo, Jack,"
Said I, as casually as anger could:
"I'll teach you one day when you've understood

---

[9]. Pronounced here as "caff", an English term for a basic eatery without airs and graces.

The elementary rules of decent manners."
He sulked all day but never cast his spanners
Again in the works, and slowly week by week,
Although I never cured his Cockney cheek,
His grossness wilted and a wiser lad
Showed something of the little wit he had.
And later when the wars had something lulled
And his remembrance of our rift had dulled
He raised the question of his judo lessons.
A judo club I knew held open sessions
On Sunday morning so Jack went along
And took to it as Welshmen take to song.

So down the register of fault and crime
Called twice a day a seeming endless time.
Garbet and Tulloch, Grogan, Bates and Ashe,
The moon-faced Murphy who had whipped the cash
Meant for the poor – and he had some excuse
For thinking it was meant for private use –
Harry who stole the scooters, Burke whose flair
For fancy shoes gave each day its own pair,
Alfonso with his glorious Afro fuzz,
Capelli who could tell what handsome does,
Greeko with wad of notes and gleaming knife,
Garnet embroidering the facts of life,
Old Reg and Thomas, Carlos, Timms and White.
Thomas had lost his right eye in a fight
Some time before I came and growing morose
And biting bitter added to his loss

What friends he had: he very seldom spoke
And almost snarled when others saw a joke.
It gives me joy what small success I had
Brought slender bonds of friendship to this lad
And that the book he gave me at the end
Bears this inscription: "To our Sir, my friend."

But saddest of them all was Peter Blair.
I learnt he was an orphan in the care
Of his grandmother, kindly fussing soul,
Oblivious of the sadly saintly role
Her grandson played each day he trudged to school.
Peter was doubtless something of a fool
To Moray House; but he'd been well brought up;[10]
Knew how to speak and walk and sup,
Control his mind and sit without a clatter,
And though the Powers dismiss of little matter
Ought but Intelligence they claim to test,
I have observed so often how the best
Slips through their fingers and smart Alec reigns[11]
With nothing but a better stock of brains.

---

[10]. Moray House was at that time a distinguished teacher training college, and is now a school within the College of Arts, Humanities and Social Science at the University of Edinburgh.

[11]. A "smart aleck", also spelled smart alek or smart alec, is someone who communicates their knowledge in an obnoxious, cocky manner, often sarcastically.

Peter knew little but he felt his lack
And bore the pilgrim's burden on his back
With wondrous stoicism against the jibes
Of false conceit and sloth, and tempting bribes
Of fellowship, and proffered lettings off
From being bashed because he was a toff.[12]
It was a humbling thing to see him wait
For crumbs of knowledge from a laden plate,
And many a time my smouldering anger flared
For very pity of one boy who cared.

Twelve of the lads had been before the Beak.[13]
In this superior blasé little clique
Those on probation marked the upper bracket,
Whose wooden strut in jeans and leather jacket
Was more pronounced: the law had marked them out
As criminals to be concerned about,
And such responsibility demanded
A tardy acquiescence when commanded
And fierce contempt for any diligence.
The rift twixt idealism and common sense
Cuts deep into the fibre of our time.
It is the main-spring of the mounting crime
That so appals; for idealists will not
Be tipped by humble toilers on the spot,
And government can never see the pity
Behind the plots and planners in committee.

Money they had in plenty and to spare
And most at Christmas-tide or when the Fair
Put up behind the Troc; then money flowed[14]
Like water and ebbed until the bare rocks showed
Amidst the running tide. And so I chose
To harness on the flood the good that goes
With opulence. I floated a school fund,
And twice a week the beggar's hat went round
For refugees and orphans, waifs and strays,
And good was done in many little ways
For giver and receiver; good and bad,
For I had more than one light-fingered lad
To cope with and correct as best I could:
So when one bumper week our total stood
At one pound twelve – the most we'd ever got –
Forbearance burst its bounds and bang the lot!
As luck would have it Reg left many clues
And as in those things there's no time to lose,
I tackled him forthwith complete with proof.
Cornered like a rat he raised the roof

---

12. "Toff" is a slang term for someone belonging to the upper classes, or more generally, anyone perceived to be of a higher social standing than the speaker.
13. "Beak" is a slang term for a judge or magistrate.
14. "Troc" is the London Trocadero, which was a restaurant on Coventry Street with a rear entrance on Shaftesbury Avenue. Built in 1896, the restaurant closed in 1965, shortly after Milton Row was written. The building has been repurposed several times since, most recently as a hotel.

With shouts and curses trooper never heard
And salvoes of a famed four-lettered word.
I heard him out then softly had my say
But ere I'd told him how he must repay
The loss and make amends to all his mates
The door crashed in and there stood Jimmy Bates.
"You bloody four-eyed bastard," blurted Jim,[15]
"I'll kick yer teeth in if y'wallop 'im.
'E's my mate, see, so keep yer paws off mister.
It weren't ole Reg. I know 'e ain't no twister."[16]
His blood was up but half of it was bluff
And t'other half the weak and watery stuff
That goes for blood among the slum-land toughs,
But I'd no mind just then for fisticuffs:
Besides, I sensed in Jim the knifing breed.
A hulking oaf, he couldn't write or read
And bore his ignorance with a sullen pride:
But come what may I had to turn the tide
Which now ran strong against my struggling rule.
I turned to Reg. "You find another school.
There is no place in this for common thieves.
And you, my boasting dandy, when he leaves
You follow suit or else apologise.
Make no mistake, I'll cut you down to size,
I'll wind your gas-bag of its blaa and bluff
And make the likes of you look small enough."
They went, somewhat abashed at this new thrust.
With 'might do', in the fury, turned to 'must'
I to the Head and tabled my request.
At first he laughed thinking it was a jest,

But quickly disabused, his face turned sour.
He wished to know who'd given me the power
To expel children presto from his school,
Then softening, commenced to drip and drool
About his worries and the unenviable task
Of keeping order, emboldening me to ask
How my request could weaken discipline.
"You must appreciate the place you're in,
And make allowances for boys like these.
Stealing is not a crime but a disease
With such like lads. Do what you can to stop it.
Tell him if there's a next time he will cop it;
But as for transfer it can not be done.
In all my years I've never given one
For misdemeanour and I'll not begin:
Best not advertise the mess you're in.
And where d'you think's the head whose such a fool
As take the throw-outs of another school?"
This final fatuous argument bore weight.
Its lack of cowardice at any rate
Commended it, and having lost the fight
I must at all cost now avoid a flight,
Must hold to every scrap of common-sense
And organise my next line of defence.
A patched-up settlement was thus devised:
My malcontents at length apologised,

---

15. "Four-eyes" is a derogatory term for someone who wears glasses.
16. "Twister" is an outdated British term for a deceitful/unscrupulous person.

But smirked with knowledge that their fake defeat
Had called my bluff and forced a fine retreat.

Pitched battles, parleys, running fights and routs,
Guerrilla tactics, truces, boxing bouts,
Resorts to reason or the riot act,
Brow-beating bully stuff and ginger tact:
Each had its moment and the moment gone
Another act be hastily put on,
For those who teach the rabble of the town
Must on the motley, ape the dauntless clown
And down the ambushed passes with a song
Press on or perish: and the way is long.
And thus the battle raged from day to day
Till wielded rod cut out a narrow way
To Reason's kingdom, and the rule of law
Dawned fitfully as I held in awe
The savage rabble who were children yet.
They learnt to listen, and the stage was set
At last for Art to work its ancient spell
And fashion from the shambles something well.
Our work was hindered and our progress slow
Because of all the facts they didn't know.
Ten years of schooling in neglected classes,
Always the bottom – so what? – always passes
To higher forms, for with our modern notion
That years can of themselves demand promotion
Our Willie feels no cold draught of disgrace:
He can afford to saunter in the race

Whose winning post keeps with him as he runs.
They do a great disservice to their sons
Who hide the truths of inequality.
Mankind can right Nature's disparity
And rise to challenge with a strengthened will,
For spirit prospers by a tempered ill
And finds a purpose in its poisoned sting.
'Twas thus the sluggish worm first took to wing
And thus shall man at last break out of mind
And go one better than our mere mankind.
And thus too Willie freed from kind deceit
Can forge a victory from a real defeat.

Slow was the progress for the grapes were sour
And every minute's lesson took an hour.
"Why should I?" greeted each polite request
And hardened to "You make me", if a test
Of strength showed promise and the chance to fight
And argue whether they or I were right.
Knowledge is clad in sober humbleness;
With well-cut ease and usage in his dress
He is himself, always at home and sure:
Ignorance, ugly as a conspicuous sewer
Upon the beach, is dolled in cheap conceit,
And fidgeting on height of fashion feet
He feels his raiment like a suit of mail.
Not greatest fault or foolishness would fail
To bring the justifying quip or moan
And all the world be wrong but they alone,

Whose arid minds and infantile belief
Turned inward like the fly-infested leaf
To wither and infect and spoil the tree.
And yet when failure registered, to me
It was they turned; no matter lack of grace
Some small assurance in a shiftless place.
But all their faults could none so much depress
My spirit as their studied commonness.
The human mass is beastly at the best
But city peasantry can lick the rest
In sheer vulgarity and villainies know-how.
Always aggrieved and spoiling for a row
They nag at life and curse and so abuse
Good things, they grow immune to all good news.
Curled up in cankered doubt, hunched up in hate,
Human response comes niggardly and late
And laughter that God meant for fellowship
Becomes as cruel and cutting as a whip.
Nothing of charm was there or charity,
Only this cultivated crude vulgarity
They flaunted with so fierce perverted pride,
And like some prehistoric monster's hide
Was their defence against a dull inanity.
Vain without cause is double vanity;
But when the canker of conceit has sprung
From nurtured filth and cultivated wrong
Then pride, puffed out of nothing million-fold,
Screams out hysterical: I'll *not* be told.

But what is simpler than to blurt out blame
And end our anger in an easy name.
The tragedy I witnessed was the trial
Of petty culprits for a crime erstwhile
Committed by the truly guilty ones.
It seldom is that those who fire the guns
Start up the war, nor were my boys to blame
For playing dirty in a dirty game.
With key around their necks they took the streets
Before they spoke: still sucking dummy teats
They joined the gang, and then from fight to fight
They learnt the jungle law that strength was right
And all the stronger for dishonesty.
One day we'll learn the mortal tragedy
Of working mother and unwanted child.
This Age has seen the family hearth defiled
By national gods of luxury and greed,
When all oblivious of a child's prime need,
Mothers have tuned their lives to factory whistles,
And English homes that had of yore been castles
Now boarding houses, bed and breakfast places,
Devoid of care, of love, of human graces
That spring from leisure at a mother's knee.
A wise dictator would make this decree:
"Mothers shall have but one exclusive care;
To singly bring to adulthood an heir
To all the wealth and wonder of the state.
And none shall shirk and none shall delegate
This duty, which is virtue's very fount,
And whose neglect is treason paramount."

Home is the branch that holds our mortal swing,
The one secure, unmoving, certain thing
That pulls the rooftops down and sets us free
To soar beyond on sinewed trust, and see
The urgent vistas endless beckoning.
The boys before me had no reckoning
Beyond the walls that bound them to the earth.
A prisoned mind was theirs by right of birth;
And might the devil in them scale the wall
No hand was there to help them should they fall.
A primitive low life of fist and curse,
Made more degenerate by a well-lined purse
And backed by Worker's rights and Welfare's care –
Whose burden other mugs are made to bear –
This was the life and the philosophy
They must accept of sad necessity
For it was home: they knew no other place.
And gaping open on each gormless face
These social sores oozed out their ugliness
To spoil and poison Nature's comeliness:
Cheap taste, suspicion, filth and prejudice,
Lies and the cult of never caring less,
The fun of knocking off and flogging quick,
The bandied jollity about the nick,
The slur that only simpletons were good,
The worship of the whores of Hollywood;
Rogues on the scrounge and rascals on the fiddle,
And every puny mind upon the riddle
Of win or draw on some far football field;
What chance had Reg or Willie but to yield?

What ideal was before them to revere?
What just authority for them to fear?

Since London first was christened 'the great wen',[17]
It has been breeding cocky little men
Who bob about like sparrows in the gutter
And never seem to fly but love to flutter.
They are a busy breed, aggressive, vain,
Filled up with self, and emptied, fill again;
They hate all learning, always know the score,
And may deny that two and two make four
If minded to: they make a song and dance
Of what's not fair, meaning what won't enhance
Their pride or pocket: they are bloody-minded,
But close as cubs with those that have befriended,
And like young cubs they paw and slap and cuff
Or suddenly go head-high in a huff.
It's hard to follow what they talk about,
For when they speak the words come tumbling out
Half-formed and hideous as a broken bell.
They think the greatest joke is speaking well.
Their virtue is a cruel continual wit
That fires away unmindful of who's hit:
At best a glory and at worst a light
Amidst the dismal city-dweller's night.

---

[17] A "wen" is an abnormal growth on the skin, such as a boil or cyst. London was first referred to by this disparaging nickname in the 1820s by radical pamphleteer and champion of rural England William Cobbett.

The priceless Cockney wit won many a day
When I had packed my case and was away
From Milton Row forever, with its grime,
Its sham pretensions, its unpunished crime,
But for the shaft of jesting joy that fell
Out of the heavens into my black hell.
"A minute's silence, blokes, for Sir's departed 'air."
And bowed each somber face in mock despair.
"'E ain't a bad ole stick", conceded one.
"But got the woodworm bad," flashed out the fun
Behind a poker face: or once demanding
A book away, in mock misunderstanding
A wag turned round to Wanker with a shout:
"Put it away, Sir? 'E ain't got it out!"

II.

Logic is but a glint in England's crown,
Whose glory flames in justice, whose renown
Glows warm in common-sense hypocrisy,
Whose fire is liberty: for logically
A politician of the Tory breed
Should follow and advance the Tory creed,
And Socialists should work for Socialism.
But no such laws of logic yet inform
The English mind nor frame its politics.
Democracy is trumps and what takes tricks
Is paramount: it is no paradox
That principles can veer like weather-cocks
And labels stick; nor is it cause for wonder
When some high Tory steals a Marxist's thunder,
Or Socialists send off their sons to Eton,
Or liberals think queer boys should be beaten.
Our English ways are like our English weather,
Each day its own and never two together.
And so it was that nineteen forty-four
Saw Socialism triumphant, and the door
On family freedom closed but to a crack
With massive wedges of the State at back.
Then was the classless commonwealth begun
And every man delivered up his son
To be instructed as the State thought fit
Strictly as experts measured out his wit.
Farewell fond parent's pride; hail National brains:
The Marxist rules if Laissez-faire still reigns;
For here we have a truly English story,
The master Socialist himself a Tory.

But though our laws are seldom what they seem
Democracy is yet man's noblest dream
And nearest to the justice men desire
Against the villainies that men conspire.
Democracy is choice and right and power
For common folk, and if we sing the flower
O'er much ere patient time has formed the fruit
Yet harvest comes if care be at the root.
Our future is such human husbandry.
Small wonder then that now I grieve to see
So much untilled and waste, so much run wild,
So much of bitter fruit, of problem child.
It is small wonder, but more wondrous yet
How powers-that-be conveniently forget
Unpleasant facts, and pompously ignore
The lengthening queue of wrongs without their door.

When Faith declines we lean upon the Law
And let Authority like some jackdaw
Issue its slogans and from beady eyes
Observe where every sparkling object lies,
Then nimbly nab it with official zest
To feather more its own fantastic nest.
We once believed in Men and no man more
Than when the roused schoolmaster took the floor
To voice decision or to punish wrong.
His word was final as a fighting gong.
Justice flowed from him luminous and clear
And reverence followed in the steps of fear.

Now is the law: the man has faded out
And bold decision fallen to shifty doubt.
The weak and visionless are sitting pretty
Well versed in every edict of committee
And positive in nothing but assent
To whatsoe'er their masters may invent:
The strong and true, watching their handwork fall
Invoke their gods but no help comes at all.
Psychiatrists wax fat and jailers curse
While every standard slips from bad to worse.
It is an age of bluff and window dressing,
Of flowery progress and official blessing;
And woe betide the worm who dare demur
At public whiting of the sepulchre.

All hierarchies are gall to living things.
They tie the feet and clip the eager wings
Of enterprise, deforming human souls
To fit them into mental pigeonholes,
And – sin of sins – misuse paternal care
By preaching love when only law is there.
Make no mistake, once Willie's through the gate
The humble teacher holds your Willie's fate.
Headmasters and Ministry men may rule
When, where and how poor Willie goes to school,
But it is in the classroom day by day
That he will learn to honour and obey,
To work and think and know, to count the cost
Of give and take, and learn to make the most

Of partial talents in imperfect times.
The discontent that fans these smouldering rhymes
Comes first of fear that in this Welfare State
A factory law shall finally dictate
The running of our schools. Inspectors thrive,
Heads of department drone in every hive,
Headmasters match their wits with paper forms,
Ministry wizards spell out trends and norms,
Psychiatrists sort out the subtle causes
Of why our Willie's life is not all roses,
Bluff politicians emanate a plan
And prophesy about the super-man
Whose skill and drive alone can see it through,
And lest the devil should not have his due
Nor Sense perform what Science cannot bless,
Each university will soon possess
A seat of criminology, upon
The which some hazy ineffectual don
Will launch his lectures and unreel his books,
Fishing the stream of crime until he hooks
The wished-for whopper that no angler yet
Has ever wholly managed to forget,
While all the time committees sit and say
They'd better sit again another day:
And all their sound and fury signifies
But this sad truth: top people *must* tell lies.
Only the humble teacher at his art
Can tell the truth and make the truth a part
Of living flesh and blood: *he* is the top
And all your office boys and all your crop

Of organising Johnnies on the wagon,
Who file St George and vote to feed the dragon.
For all their pomp and power are trappings merely.
And where have trappings yet been bought so dearly!

Law is the darling of the empowered weak.
By jot and tittle of fine rules they seek
Mankind's salvation in a Statute Book:
And many the honest man to end a crook
Who must traverse the labyrinthine way
That adds a legal obstacle a day.
The institution of the cane and book
Is one such dish committees love to cook.
Record in full the name of each offender,
Note next the date, the age, the form; then render
The brief particulars of each offence,
How oft administered and where and whence,
And having signed the whole, return with cane
For counter signature, till used again.
This register of failure – it is held
The cane is failure and the master failed –
Must be inspected by the Governors
Who have the right to pose the whys and wherefores,
And since advance attends their satisfaction
Is it a wonder punishment's on ration?
Is it a marvel human flesh and blood
Is partial to the cheque and spares the rod?
And is it strange that Willie twigs the flaw
And baulks his betters by appeal to law?

On no account must any teacher cuff
Or slap or shake a child: such barbarous stuff
Is out of keeping with our modern ways;
It is a relic of the bad old days
Which only black reactionaries invoke,[18]
And then – to sober those who see the joke –
The iron fist fills out beneath the glove
And violence invades this reign of love:
"Infringement of this rule shall mean dismissal."
Can you not hear the pedagogue's low whistle
As he lets Willie go his merry way
And punishment takes second place to pay?

Never since Idealism first set her face
To lure Reality from his right place
Beside plain Fact and lead him fancy free
Have they together set on such a spree.
I've seen the inkwells fly, the windows smashed,
The polished tops of fine new tables gashed,
Books that were spanking new ripped into shreds,
Great hulking louts hold pistols to the heads
Of timid College girls who'd had the pluck
To slap their faces when told, "Go and fuck."
I've seen a conscientious master spat on,
Reports of monstrous misdemeanours sat on

---

[18]. This refers to the authoritarian regimes of President Nkrumah of Ghana 1960–66, President Nyerere of Tanzania 1962–85, and Prime Minister/President Obote of Uganda 1962–71.

By spineless watchdogs too afraid to bark,
Lest they betray their motto – 'Keep it dark'.
I've seen the bullies triumph, liars win;
Young teachers, six months after coming in,
Grown sick at heart and cynical in mind
Because Authority is deaf and blind
To blatant faults and wicked crying wrongs;
I've seen illiterates slouch out in throngs
To meet the modern world at fair fifteen
And shocked employers wonder where they've been;
I've seen enough to know that only lies
Bring power and place, and year by year the cries
In the wilderness grow fewer and more faint
Till some calm fury of the common saint
Be needful ere defeat avoid despair
And seeing no promise come, yet still to care.
Say 'Yes' and prosper: 'No' will never do
To fill a wallet or to head the queue
For office plums deft fingered from the pie.
Success knows one refrain, 'How good am I!'
And Mammon seldom stints a hand to bless
The willing toady who will stick to 'Yes'.
Fear is the father of our cares and striving,
The dear dread bogey of our civilising
That haunts the halls of order and success
And makes a god of sorts in some sort bless
The sad creation of our common hands.
Respect and reverence which fear commands
Are cornerstones in all this world's upraising,
And yet the chorus of our pundits praising

The fall of Fear, with all his legions fled
And all his wicked works discredited,
Grows daily louder and is only drowned
By shrieking hooligans at last unbound.
Bankers are shot and grandmas get the cosh
Because of all the silly half-baked bosh
That stands for education in our schools.
A teacher works with two essential tools:
Knowledge, and power to make that knowledge break
All barriers down, till for its own sweet sake
It comes a guest to one-time hostile minds.
Not till self-pleased Authority unbinds
The hands of teachers, scraps its checks and cults,
And seeks the one essential thing – results –
Will Education flare to life again
And fire a beacon on the faults of men.
An end of reasoned choice and lax response:
Let things be done if they are asked for once.
Less rummaging for cause, more rods for cure:
A little fear can make a harlot pure.
Less worship of the brain and more of guts:
The living opens when the learning shuts.
Less expert knowledge, more parental doubt:
Who lives the life knows best what it's about.
More faith in men and less in bits of paper:
Our God is yet a personal Creator.
People before and principles behind:
Man was not made for pigeonholes of mind.
Less fine abstractions, more of faulty blood:
Only the human act is bad or good.

Less affluence now, more thrift for future time:
The life is not in riches but in rhyme.
Less take, more give: less grudge, more saving grace:
The mask of learning's yet a kindly face.
A ban on bigness; let's have little schools
Where children's brains are something more than tools
For national purposes. Set learning free
From bonds of Science and Technology.
Less talk of brick and mortar, more of mind:
A place to learn in is not hard to find.
Less faith in letters fluttering from a name:
The trumps are Fortune's gift in every game.
Less love of office, more of service given:
A little child gave man a glimpse of heaven.
Less outward show and more of inner worth,
That music of true learning fill the earth
With Truth and Beauty in such harmony
That Life itself become a symphony.

Happy the land, inviolate the home,
And both brought nearest yet to kingdom come,
Where love of learning dwells. It does not grow
Unnurtured, but with pruning-hook and hoe
And constant labour and unstinted love
The bud will blossom and the bloom improve,
And only at the gardener's greening hand
Shall flower and fruit luxuriate the land.
We are but human but our being wings
In spirit flight above material things.

A fallen Angel or a Son of God,
The foot of Progress in the land untrod,
A clever brute, a conscience-bidden beast,
Divine ambassador or Nature's priest;
Whate'er the theory – this is always true:
The only meaning lies twixt me and you.
No value, virtue, vision of an end
Commensurate with spirit can pretend
To lie in aught but man's regard for man.
The human army marches, and the van[19]
Must be its teachers, daring, faithful, sure,
Watchful in ease and willing to endure,
Strong-willed as iron, fine as filigree,
Single of mind, in operation free
Of detailed orders and mass discipline,
Happy to lose that lesser men may win.
First and first-hand they measure up the foe.
The High Command must gauge and guess: they know.
And all the host behind them wait the hour
When knowledge floods the rising tide of power
And in the vision of a thing to be
Come on in faith and gain the victory.

---

[19] "Van" is used here as shorthand for "vanguard"; the foremost part of an advancing force, leading the way.

III.

The day began like any other day.
First registration then the give-away
Of milk, abandoned with an affluent sip
For Joe the Keeper to remove and tip
Straight in the drain; then worship in the hall,
Where half a dozen hymn-books were let fall
And half a hundred pearls of truth divine
Were flung in handfuls to the grunting swine.
And prayers performed the canticle of blame,
With but a few refinements was the same.
Another lavatory seat had disappeared,
The cloak-room towels had once again been smeared,
Two more new overcoats were razor-ripped,
And some bright budding scientist had tipped
Sulphuric acid on Miss Wooder's flowers.
But as a clock chimes out the quarter hours
Heard but unheeded, this recital fell
On stony ground, for it was known full well
Few culprits had been caught and those that were
Waxed cynical that tick-offs might deter
Their daring, and repeated the offence.
With Service over, classes could commence
In earnest, but I'd scarce set my lot down
When in walked the headmaster with a frown;
Would I go to his room and pacify
An irate parent: he had had a try
But seemingly the fault was somehow mine,
Though what or how he could not yet divine.
I found a little grubby-shirted man
Who, ere I'd introduced myself, began

A wild tirade 'gainst every other race
And would I like it were I in his place.
"You fink the sun shines from their arse-'oles, mate.
If you'd a tenth the trouble on your plate
They've put on mine you'd change yer bloody tune.
My doorstep's like a bloody beer saloon
Morning and night wiv 'em bone idle swine.
And if they'd mind their business I'd mind mine,
But my own missus can't get through the door
Wivout some bastard takes her for an 'ore.
It's fine for you to air yer 'oly stuff,
But I live wiv it, mate. I've 'ad enough.
Calypsos may be fine, but Kitekat
Stinks out the bloody bedroom in our flat.
D'ye fink your missus would enjoy the job
Of cleaning up some filthy slimy gob
From off 'er doorstep? You blokes make me sick.
Wot 'em bloody lot wants is one good kick
Right up the arse and out of it for good
Before they ruin every neighbourhood."
And on and on, till half his fury spent,
I thrust a query if his words were meant
For me at all, for I recalled no cause.
It was a touch and in the virgin pause
I drove it home that I was unaware
Of whom he spoke, of what offence or where
Committed, but he cast a look to kill.
"You know wot you've bin on at to our Bill.
'Ain't no such thing as race' says 'e! That's you.
I reckon, matie, you're a bloody Jew."

And with this final sally he was gone.
What the occasion or which Bill his son
I never knew, but somewhere seed was sown
And some remark of mine had struck and grown
And struggled sunward on a hostile soil.

Back in my room I found a wild turmoil
With Bates and Fordham scrapping on the floor
Amid a circle greedy-eyed for gore
And raucous in the coarse delight of fists.
I waded in, grabbing a pair of wrists
And tugged apart a twisted beastly mess.
A Solon might be pardoned should he guess[20]
That such a broil must argue deadly hurt
To life or limb or honour at the start,
But when the law prevailed and truth was out
It proved the mortal struggle was about
A stub of pencil claimed on either hand
Though new ones were given gratis on demand.

In all professions there are chores that grate
On dignity, and each their own relate
Ad infinitum in a lay-world's ears
Till curses fall that had intended tears.

---

[20]. "Solon" is a term that can refer to any wise lawgiver, though here the author may be referring specifically to the Athenian statesman, constitutional lawmaker and poet of that name (c. 630 – c. 560 BC) from whom the term originated.

School meals provide the teacher's hobby-horse,
And every staffroom finds a way to curse
The dinner duty: thus we used to call
Our imposition the pig-sty patrol.
It was my turn, and late, I heard the babble
Burst in a roar and knew I'd hit on trouble.
A crafty catapulted lump of meat
Had scored a hit on Cook's caught-bending seat,
Who, on her dignity and hot to blame –
Though knowing nothing but the line of aim –
Seized on a meatless plate as certain proof:
But Tulloch, whose it was, remained aloof
From her wild ranting, and would not admit it.
"I ate it, matie. If you like I'll shit it,"
He grunted in a solemn monotone;
And Cook, though by her nature never prone
To aught but verbal scolding, took the ring,
And I was audience to that wondrous thing
A cook and customer in mortal fight.
The greens and gravy splattered left and right,
The crocks went crashing and the irons clanged
And wild supporters bawled their hopes and banged
The tabletops, rooting their choice to win.
The cook had weight and she was wading in
But Tulloch had the style and danced away
And would on points have carried off the day
Had not a greased potato brought him down
Leaving for Cook the undisputed crown
And lusty seconds to lift high her arms
And mid renewed excursions and alarms

Hoist her on high and march towards the door.
T'were vanity to order or implore
In such a strait, so with such speed I might
I raced towards the gate and shut it tight;
Then with my back against it turned aside
The march triumphal, or I fear the ride
Of our pop Cook had compassed half the town.
But once around the playground brought her down,
Flushed from her sudden dizzy rise to fame
Yet flattered just enough to mellow blame
And list her service in restoring law.
The knock-out was a left hook to the jaw
The rumour went and though the rumour lied
Cook was too wise a bird to have denied
So good an ally so she let it grow.
Her stock was up and she would keep it so.

The afternoon began with bustling out
My chairs and tables: I'd forgot about
The Case Committee, who'd come fluttering in
Soon after two, all eager to begin;
For every month my classroom cleaned its face,
Rouged its pale lips and powdered o'er each trace
Of wrinkled strife, and combed its tangled hair.
You'd see a merry change would make you stare.
A gush of welfare women, bent on good,
Possessed that Willie's case be understood,
Scrabble and scrape o'er records and reports,
Cackle of after-care and cluck of courts,

Gobble at facts and peck offending combs
Over the dunghills of unhappy homes,
While some puffed rooster struts and preens and crows
In admiration of the lot he knows
All cock-a-hoop with all the harem his
Like some headmaster – which, of course, he is.
The Fishman scandal, like a sudden fox –
Though only one of many violent shocks –
Had kept them in a huddle now for hours.
It was a case to shatter ivory towers.
'Fishmans' was as familiar as the sun
And to this dingy Mecca everyone
At Milton Row made daily pilgrimage
For smokes and chews and ought on printed page
That yielded profit, which was small enough,
Newspapers, comics and the shoddy stuff
That simple literacy has interest in.
Ma Fishman was cadaverous and thin:
Fishman himself rotund and bluff and hale,
But Fate concealed a sting within its tail
And latterly had cruelly struck him down
With polio. One side from toe to crown
Was paralysed and he was now quite dumb.
Yet far from being dispirited or glum
His quick brown eyes were always filled with fun
And he would wave his hand at everyone
Jesting in signs or jogging his wife's mind
On current prices or the usual kind
Of tea that this or that old lady had.
Their only son was still an undergrad

At Kings, and they had long-laid plans to move
When he was finished, to the peace of Hove.
A busy Friday through and shutters up
The Fishmans had at last retired to sup
Into the quiet room behind the shop.
For twelve hours on her feet and fit to drop
Ma Fishman busied yet o'er stove and sink
Oblivious that through a curtain chink
Eyes were upon her and the moment near
When shock of sudden violence would sear
Two hearts in terror that now mused in peace.
Courts in their cold decisions never cease
To miss the point because they miss the pain,
And that the bond that tied these ageing twain
Should twist and tighten in a mutual dread
And dangle Death henceforth above each head
Was nothing relevant: lawless acts
Bring from the magistrate a call for facts,
Which bold recital told how sudden attack
On Mrs Fishman flung her on her back
Where she was gagged and bound, dragged on a chair
Beside her husband and the helpless pair
Subjected to a hell of blow and curse
And flashing knives that threatened something worse
By three intruders masked, but plainly young,
Of whom one heartless specimen had sung
A pop-tune while his pals ransacked the place,
Beating the rhythm out on each victim's face.
Their haul was small enough – some paltry pence –
Found in the till, making no kind of sense

Of their vile violence or the damage done.
It was in their warped minds 'a bit of fun'.

Sibson, a throw-out from a grammar school
Had come to Milton Row and played the fool
In several classes ere he sank to mine.
Quicker than most he'd learnt to toe the line,
But only in externals: underneath
He was rebellious, muttering in his teeth
And always on the brink of misdemeanour.
Twice I had warned him for his bad behaviour,
But his conceit had grown to such a size
That all but what it fed on he thought lies
And his resolve to go his own sweet way
Without correction and with no delay
So much possessed him and so closed his eyes
To his well-being, shock and not surprise
Was my reaction when the news came out
That my bright Sibson was the very lout
Who'd flashed the flick-knife in the corner shop.

Time was when such a wicked crime would stop
The very heartbeat of Society,
But in these barbarous times the moiety
Of common men are so bemused by crime
They take it like the fancy of a dream
Before the waking; and yet others wake
Under the spell of dreams they cannot break
And gild reality with fancy's failing:
Only the few cry out and unavailing

Shake off the slumber from their threatened day.
The Sibsons, knowing this, are undismayed
By consequences of their heinous crimes.
They are but restless children of the times
Blown by the wind of change and free of guilt
Though they should drive their vices to the hilt.
Not sorrow then or shame, but sour elation
At being bad and pride to have probation.
For status with the boys was Sibson's feeling.

Was it a wonder then I hit the ceiling
When he was brought protesting from the yard
For having razor blades – which school rules barred –
And ripping into shreds a fellow's blazer.
"I bought 'em lunch-time for me ole man's razor,"
He bawled at me, and hearing it fall lame,
"You always pick on me. I get the blame
Because them sodding scum-bags was beat up."
And tolerance at last forbore to stop
Instinctive justice: as my heart's core sank
Into the last despair of Anna Frank
And all the bones of Belsen piled on high
Rose up before me and blacked out the sky
I struck the boy.
                The rest is easy told.
The Sister, who professed to be appalled
At such brutality, stuck plaster on,
Informed superiors, and thereupon
The grim legality of County Hall,
Intending nothing but entailing all,

Finished my teaching life in London Schools.
An earlier self had flung the challenge 'Fools'
And armed for battle, but I must confess
Too many costly failures to redress
Official wrongs, lost stomach for a fight
Against battalions who were always right.
And this, beyond the failing power to spread
A love of learning, is the final dread
Behind these rhymes. A glut of government
Has dulled incentive and the zeal is spent
That makes each single life an enterprise
Wherein the purpose of the living lies.
We *have* gone to the ant, and her low ways
Inform the ordered folly of our days.
The rebel wilts, the hue of passion fades
And Christian souls revert to Classic shades.
The creeping death of peace at any price
Destroys the spirit, sick of cowardice;
And failing strength, content to lessen pain,
Dreams of a health whose hopes are ever vain.
The final afternoon was strangely long.
The sense of earnest gloom did not belong
To my 4B, and I was frankly glad
When shortly after play the chosen lad
Rose to his feet and fired the parting words.
That I should have a gift was on the cards;
But I expected handkerchiefs or socks
Or after-shaving lotion: when a box
Of staggering size was lugged along the floor,
Though I had suffered classroom gifts galore,

A mixture of suspicion and suspense
Possessed me. It was not for long: at once
The stage was taken by the bustling Sid
Who fell upon his knees and ripped the lid
And heaved upon my desk a splendid case.
Relief and pleasure must have lit my face.
"You 'ave a decko, Sir," the chorus sang
And there before me when the catches sprang
A glutted treasure chest of gaudy wealth
Bulged up at me: "To Sir's Good Health"
A labelled Guinness read, and lotion, soap,
A hair-restorer bottle with "Some 'ope"
Across it, two outrageous ties, red socks,
A pen and pencil in a plushy box,
Cuff-links and handkerchiefs, all cheek and jowl
With bumper tins of fruit and fish and fowl,
Baked beans and coffee, ketchup, salad-cream
And endless bric-a-brac without a name:
Withal a motley for a fairground stall
And I, incredulous, the cause of all.
A silence fell. Had I not understood?
"The lot's for you Sir, cos you learned us good,"
Sid proffered: and the pity of it struck.
The pain and pity, and – it dawned – the luck.

My journey to the bus perforce was slow
That evening. Sombre thoughts of Milton Row
Weighed on my mind as heavy as the gift
That favoured me and was so hard to lift:

And fellow-travelling with my genuine grieving
The fear that I was guilty of receiving
Dogged my slow progress in the gathering gloom.
And later, with the booty safely home,
A fog of sadness wrapped my thought about,
Thwarting my every effort to look out
And find a bearing. Everywhere a blank:
Till into drowsy reverie I sank
Telling myself the tale its long length through
Which I have yet again now told to you.

Acknowledgements

We would like to thank Maurice Reeve for believing that our father's poem, *Milton Row*, deserved a wider audience and was worthy of publication. We also thank our cousin Elizabeth Newlands for typing up the manuscript and for putting us in touch with Mary Anne Newlands Case, whom we met in New York in June 2019 to discuss the illustrations for the poem. Mary Anne and Robert have a common ancestor, George Newlands (1727–1804) and his wife Isobel Knight of Forgieside in Banffshire, North-East Scotland. Thanks also to Robert's granddaughters, Tamsin and Louise, for proofreading the manuscript and collating the material, and finally to Jamie McGarry for considering *Milton Row* a fine addition to the publications of Valley Press and for his unwavering support in making this happen.

– Peter and Simon Newlands